DISCOVERING THE COMPREHENSIVE SYSTEM OF KUK SOOL WON

Tracing Its Historical Path, Mastery of Techniques, and Practical Defense Skills

By

Author:

Whalen Kwon-Ling

Contributor:

Thomas H. Fletcher

Discovering the Comprehensive System of Kuk Sool Won

"Discovering the Comprehensive System of Kuk Sool Won" is an insightful exploration into the rich and multifaceted world of Kuk Sool Won, a traditional Korean martial art. This book takes readers on a journey through the origins and evolution of this discipline, tracing its roots back to ancient Korean martial practices and its development into the sophisticated system it is today. It delves into the philosophical underpinnings of Kuk Sool Won, emphasizing the importance of harmony, respect, and self-discipline that are central to its practice.

The book meticulously details the principles and techniques that form the core of Kuk Sool Won. It covers a broad spectrum of training methodologies, from basic stances and strikes to advanced joint locks and pressure point techniques. Readers will gain a comprehensive understanding of the rank and promotion system, learning how practitioners progress through various levels of expertise and the rigorous training involved at each stage.

One of the highlights of this book is its thorough examination of forms and patterns, known as Hyung. These are intricate sequences of movements that encapsulate the essence of Kuk Sool Won's techniques and principles. The book provides clear and detailed descriptions of these forms, making it an invaluable resource for both beginners and advanced students.

Self-defense is a crucial aspect of Kuk Sool Won, and this book offers an in-depth look at the diverse range of defensive techniques taught within the system. From practical self-defense strategies to the use of traditional Korean weapons, the book covers it all. It also explores the healing arts associated with Kuk Sool Won, including acupressure, herbal medicine, and internal energy cultivation practices that promote overall health and well-being.

In addition to its historical and technical content, "Discovering the Comprehensive System of Kuk Sool Won" discusses the modern applications and adaptations of this martial art. It shows how Kuk Sool Won has been integrated into contemporary fitness regimes and its relevance in today's fast-paced world. The book also touches on the presence of Kuk Sool

Won in popular culture, highlighting its portrayal in movies, television, and other media.

Overall, this book serves as a definitive guide for anyone interested in Kuk Sool Won, offering a wealth of knowledge in a detailed yet accessible manner. Whether you are a martial artist looking to deepen your understanding or a curious reader fascinated by Korean culture, "Discovering the Comprehensive System of Kuk Sool Won" provides an enriching and comprehensive overview of this unique martial art.

Table of Content

Introduction

Kuk Sool Won is a comprehensive Korean martial art that integrates various techniques and traditions from Korean martial arts history. It focuses on self-discipline, self-defense, and physical fitness. Kuk

Sool Won combines elements from different martial arts styles, including striking, throwing, grappling, and joint locks. This makes it versatile and effective for practitioners of all ages and skill levels.

The history of Kuk Sool Won dates back hundreds of years, drawing from ancient Korean martial traditions. It includes influences from Korean royal court martial arts, Buddhist temple martial arts, and tribal martial arts. This rich heritage is preserved and passed down through generations of practitioners. Each technique in Kuk Sool Won has a historical and cultural significance, connecting modern practitioners to their roots.

The practice of Kuk Sool Won starts with learning basic movements and stances. These foundational skills are essential for mastering more complex techniques. Beginners are taught how to stand, move, and balance correctly. This helps build strength and flexibility while preventing injuries. As students progress, they learn a variety of strikes, kicks, and blocks.

Kuk Sool Won emphasizes the importance of mental discipline alongside physical training. Practitioners are encouraged to develop focus, concentration, and a calm mind. This mental aspect is crucial for mastering advanced techniques and performing under pressure. Meditation and breathing exercises are often incorporated into training to enhance mental clarity and control.

In addition to striking techniques, Kuk Sool Won includes joint locks and grappling. These techniques are used to control and subdue opponents without causing unnecessary harm. Joint locks involve manipulating an opponent's joints to create pain and compliance. Grappling techniques involve throws and takedowns to bring an opponent to the ground.

One unique aspect of Kuk Sool Won is its emphasis on weapons training. Practitioners learn to use a variety of traditional Korean weapons, including swords, staffs, and spears. Weapons training enhances coordination, precision, and understanding of martial principles. It also provides a historical context, as many of these weapons were used by Korean warriors in the past.

Another important component of Kuk Sool Won is acrobatics and falling techniques. Practitioners learn how to fall safely to minimize injury during training or self-defense situations. Acrobatics, such as flips and rolls, improve agility and body control. These skills are not only practical but also add an exciting element to demonstrations and performances.

Kuk Sool Won promotes overall health and well-being. Regular practice improves cardiovascular fitness, strength, flexibility, and balance. It also helps reduce stress and improve mental health. The holistic approach of Kuk Sool Won means that it benefits both the body and the mind, making it a well-rounded form of exercise.

The ranking system in Kuk Sool Won is designed to motivate and track progress. Students start as white belts and advance through various colored belts until reaching black belt status. Each belt level represents a new level of skill and knowledge. Testing for each belt involves demonstrating proficiency in techniques, forms, and sparring.

Instructors in Kuk Sool Won are highly trained and certified. They guide students through their martial arts journey with patience and expertise. Instructors emphasize respect, discipline, and humility in their teaching. This creates a supportive and positive learning environment for all students.

Kuk Sool Won is practiced by people of all ages and backgrounds. It is suitable for children, adults, and seniors, each benefiting in different ways. Children develop discipline, focus, and self-confidence. Adults improve fitness, stress management, and self-defense skills. Seniors enhance mobility, balance, and mental sharpness.

The community aspect of Kuk Sool Won is also significant. Practitioners often form strong bonds with their fellow students and instructors. This sense of community provides encouragement and support, making the practice more enjoyable. Many schools and dojangs (training halls) also organize social events, seminars, and competitions.

Kuk Sool Won is recognized worldwide and has a growing number of practitioners. Its comprehensive approach to martial arts and its focus on tradition and discipline appeal to many people. The martial art continues to evolve while maintaining its historical roots. This balance of tradition and innovation keeps Kuk Sool Won relevant and exciting.

Training in Kuk Sool Won requires dedication and commitment. Practitioners are encouraged to set goals and work steadily towards them. Progress may be slow at times, but perseverance is key. The journey of learning Kuk Sool Won is as important as the destination.

The benefits of Kuk Sool Won extend beyond physical skills. Practitioners often find that the principles learned in training apply to other areas of life. Discipline, focus, and resilience are valuable traits in any endeavor. The martial art fosters personal growth and a positive attitude.

In conclusion, Kuk Sool Won is a rich and diverse martial art that offers numerous benefits. Its combination of physical techniques, mental discipline, and cultural heritage makes it unique. Whether for self-defense, fitness, or personal development, Kuk Sool Won provides a rewarding and enriching experience for all who practice it.

Historical Background

The history of Kuk Sool Won is deeply rooted in the martial traditions of Korea, spanning over several centuries. This martial art integrates techniques from various Korean fighting styles, reflecting the rich cultural heritage of the Korean peninsula. By understanding the historical background of Kuk Sool Won, one can appreciate the depth and complexity of this martial art.

Kuk Sool Won traces its origins to ancient Korean martial arts, practiced by the Korean people for self-defense, hunting, and military training. These early techniques were influenced by the need to protect villages and families from invaders and wild animals. Over time, these techniques were refined and passed down through generations, forming the foundation of what would become Kuk Sool Won.

During the Three Kingdoms period in Korea, from approximately 57 BC to 668 AD, martial arts began to develop more formally. Each of the three kingdoms—Goguryeo, Baekje, and Silla—had its own unique fighting techniques and strategies. Martial arts were used extensively by soldiers and warriors, and training was an essential part of military preparation.

This period saw the rise of various martial traditions that would later influence Kuk Sool Won.

The Silla Kingdom, in particular, played a significant role in the development of Korean martial arts. The Hwarang, an elite group of young warriors, were trained in various martial disciplines, including archery, swordsmanship, and hand-to-hand combat. The Hwarang were not only skilled fighters but also adhered to a strict code of ethics, emphasizing loyalty, courage, and honor. The teachings and techniques of the Hwarang greatly influenced the development of Kuk Sool Won.

Following the unification of the Korean peninsula under the Silla Kingdom, martial arts continued to evolve. The subsequent Goryeo Dynasty, which lasted from 918 to 1392, saw further refinement and formalization of martial arts. During this time, the military played a crucial role in maintaining the stability and security of the kingdom. Martial arts training became more organized, with a focus on both individual combat skills and group tactics.

The Goryeo Dynasty is also notable for the introduction of Buddhism to Korea. Buddhist monks, who often traveled between Korea, China, and Japan, brought with them various martial techniques. These monks incorporated martial arts into their training, blending physical discipline with spiritual practice. The influence of Buddhist martial arts is evident in many of the techniques and philosophies of Kuk Sool Won.

The Joseon Dynasty, which followed the Goryeo Dynasty and lasted from 1392 to 1897, continued to build on the martial traditions of Korea. The Joseon government established a centralized military training system, known as the "Mugyo," which aimed to standardize martial arts training across the kingdom. This period saw the compilation of various martial arts manuals, documenting techniques and strategies. These manuals served as important references for future generations of martial artists.

One of the most significant contributions of the Joseon Dynasty to martial arts was the development of the "Muyedobotongji," a comprehensive martial arts manual compiled in the late 18th century. This manual included detailed descriptions and illustrations of various martial techniques, including weapons training, hand-to-hand combat, and grappling. The Muyedobotongji is considered one of the most important historical documents related to Korean martial arts and has had a lasting impact on the development of Kuk Sool Won.

Throughout the centuries, martial arts in Korea were not only practiced by soldiers and warriors but also by civilians. Village militias and local self-defense groups often trained in martial arts to protect their communities. These practices helped to preserve and pass down martial traditions, ensuring that they remained an integral part of Korean culture.

In addition to the practical applications of martial arts, there was also a strong cultural and spiritual component. Many martial arts techniques were influenced by Confucian and Buddhist philosophies, which emphasized moral integrity, discipline, and self-control. These principles are deeply embedded in the practice of Kuk Sool Won, reflecting the holistic approach to martial arts training.

The 20th century brought significant changes to Korea, including Japanese occupation from 1910 to 1945. During this period, traditional Korean martial arts were suppressed, and many practitioners had to practice in secret. Despite these challenges, the knowledge and techniques of Korean martial arts were preserved by dedicated masters and practitioners. After Korea regained its independence, there was a resurgence of interest in traditional martial arts, leading to the formalization and promotion of various styles.

In 1958, Suh In-Hyuk founded Kuk Sool Won as a formal martial art, drawing on his extensive knowledge of traditional Korean martial techniques. Suh In-Hyuk sought to create a comprehensive system that integrated the diverse martial traditions of Korea. His efforts led to the establishment of Kuk Sool Won as a distinct and recognized martial art, with a structured curriculum and ranking system.

Kuk Sool Won has continued to grow and evolve since its founding. It has spread internationally, with schools and practitioners around the world. The martial art maintains a strong emphasis on tradition, while also adapting to modern training methods and needs. This balance of historical preservation and contemporary practice is one of the defining features of Kuk Sool Won.

In conclusion, the historical background of Kuk Sool Won is rich and multifaceted, reflecting the diverse influences and traditions of Korean martial arts. From its ancient roots to its formalization in the 20th century, Kuk Sool Won embodies the cultural, philosophical, and practical aspects of Korea's martial heritage. Understanding this history enhances the appreciation of Kuk Sool Won and its significance as a comprehensive martial art.

Philosophical Foundations

Kuk Sool Won is built on a strong foundation of philosophical principles. These principles guide practitioners not only in their martial arts training but also in their daily lives. They emphasize the development of both the mind and body, fostering a balanced and harmonious way of living. This holistic approach is central to the philosophy of Kuk Sool Won.

One of the key philosophical foundations of Kuk Sool Won is respect. Respect is fundamental to all interactions within the martial art. Practitioners show respect to their instructors, fellow students, and even their opponents. This respect extends beyond the training hall and into everyday life. It promotes harmonious relationships and a positive community spirit.

Another important principle in Kuk Sool Won is humility. Practitioners are encouraged to remain humble, regardless of their skill level or achievements. Humility involves recognizing one's own limitations and constantly striving for improvement. It helps prevent arrogance and fosters a learning mindset. This humility is essential for personal growth and development.

Self-discipline is a core tenet of Kuk Sool Won. Practitioners must maintain consistent training habits and adhere to the rules and etiquette of the martial art. Self-discipline involves controlling one's impulses and staying focused on long-term goals. This discipline is crucial for mastering techniques and achieving progress. It also translates into other areas of life, such as work and personal relationships.

Another significant aspect of Kuk Sool Won's philosophy is perseverance. Practitioners are taught to persist through challenges and setbacks. Perseverance means not giving up when faced with difficulties. It involves maintaining a positive attitude and continuing to put in effort, even when progress seems slow. This quality helps practitioners overcome obstacles and achieve their goals.

The concept of integrity is also central to Kuk Sool Won. Practitioners are expected to act with honesty and uphold strong moral principles. Integrity involves being truthful, fair, and ethical in all actions. This principle is important for building trust and credibility within the martial arts community and beyond. It helps create a culture of honesty and accountability.

Balance is another key philosophical foundation in Kuk Sool Won. Balance refers to the harmonious integration of mind, body, and spirit. Practitioners strive to achieve physical balance through their training, which enhances coordination and stability. Mental balance involves maintaining focus and clarity of thought. Spiritual balance encompasses a sense of inner peace and harmony. This holistic approach promotes overall well-being.

The principle of loyalty is highly valued in Kuk Sool Won. Practitioners are loyal to their instructors, peers, and the martial art itself. Loyalty involves dedication and commitment to the practice and community. It helps build strong bonds and a sense of belonging. This loyalty extends to the values and traditions of Kuk Sool Won, preserving its rich heritage.

Courage is another important principle in Kuk Sool Won. Practitioners are encouraged to face challenges and confront fears with bravery. Courage involves taking risks and stepping out of one's comfort zone. It is essential for personal growth and development. This principle helps practitioners build confidence and resilience.

Compassion is also a key aspect of Kuk Sool Won's philosophy. Practitioners are taught to be kind and considerate towards others. Compassion involves understanding and empathy. It encourages helping others and contributing positively to the community. This principle promotes a supportive and nurturing environment.

The principle of patience is emphasized in Kuk Sool Won. Practitioners learn that progress takes time and effort. Patience involves enduring difficulties and waiting for results without frustration. It is essential for mastering complex techniques and achieving long-term goals. This quality also helps practitioners remain calm and composed in various situations.

Another philosophical foundation of Kuk Sool Won is harmony. Practitioners strive to achieve harmony within themselves and with others. Harmony involves aligning actions, thoughts, and emotions. It promotes a sense of peace and cooperation. This principle is important for creating a positive and supportive training environment.

Focus is a crucial principle in Kuk Sool Won. Practitioners are trained to concentrate fully on their techniques and training. Focus involves directing one's attention and energy towards a specific goal. It is essential for achieving precision and effectiveness in martial arts. This principle also enhances productivity and efficiency in daily life.

Another significant principle is gratitude. Practitioners are encouraged to be thankful for the opportunities and support they receive. Gratitude involves appreciating the efforts of instructors, peers, and the Kuk Sool Won community. It fosters a positive and appreciative mindset. This principle helps practitioners remain humble and grounded.

The concept of mindfulness is integral to Kuk Sool Won. Practitioners are taught to be present and aware in each moment. Mindfulness involves paying attention to one's thoughts, emotions, and surroundings. It enhances self-awareness and self-control. This principle is essential for effective training and personal development.

The principle of adaptability is also important in Kuk Sool Won. Practitioners learn to adjust to changing situations and challenges. Adaptability involves being flexible and open-minded. It helps practitioners respond effectively to different scenarios. This quality is crucial for success in both martial arts and life.

Responsibility is a key principle in Kuk Sool Won. Practitioners are encouraged to take ownership of their actions and decisions. Responsibility involves being accountable and reliable. It helps build trust and respect within the community. This principle promotes a strong sense of duty and commitment.

The principle of unity is emphasized in Kuk Sool Won. Practitioners work together as a team and support each other. Unity involves cooperation and collaboration. It helps build a strong and cohesive community. This principle is important for achieving common goals and fostering a sense of belonging.

The concept of honor is also central to Kuk Sool Won. Practitioners are taught to uphold the dignity and values of the martial art. Honor involves behaving with respect and integrity. It is essential for maintaining the reputation and traditions of Kuk Sool Won. This principle helps practitioners develop a strong moral character.

In conclusion, the philosophical foundations of Kuk Sool Won encompass a wide range of principles that guide practitioners in their martial arts training and daily lives. These principles emphasize respect, humility, self-discipline, perseverance, integrity, balance, loyalty, courage, compassion, patience, harmony, focus, gratitude, mindfulness, adaptability, responsibility, unity, and honor. Together, they create a holistic and balanced approach to personal development and well-being. Understanding and embracing these principles is essential for fully appreciating and benefiting from the practice of Kuk Sool Won.

Principles and Techniques

Kuk Sool Won incorporates a vast array of principles and techniques that form the core of its practice. These elements combine to create a comprehensive martial art that addresses self-defense, physical fitness, and mental discipline. Each principle and technique has a specific purpose and function, contributing to the overall effectiveness of the martial art.

One of the fundamental principles in Kuk Sool Won is the proper stance. The stance is the foundation of all techniques, providing balance and stability. Practitioners learn various stances, each suited to different situations and movements. A solid stance ensures that a practitioner can move efficiently and maintain control during techniques.

Striking techniques in Kuk Sool Won include punches, kicks, and open-hand strikes. These techniques are designed to deliver powerful and precise blows to an opponent. Practitioners learn to generate power from their entire body, using proper mechanics and alignment. Striking involves not only strength but also speed and accuracy.

Blocking techniques are equally important in Kuk Sool Won. Practitioners learn to defend against incoming attacks using their arms and legs. Blocks can redirect or stop the force of an opponent's strike. Effective blocking requires timing, coordination, and an understanding of the opponent's movements. These techniques are crucial for self-defense.

Joint locks are another key aspect of Kuk Sool Won. These techniques involve manipulating an opponent's joints to create pain and compliance. Joint locks can be applied to various parts of the body, such as the wrists, elbows, and shoulders. They are effective for controlling an opponent without causing permanent injury. Practitioners must learn precision and control to apply these techniques safely.

Throwing techniques in Kuk Sool Won are used to unbalance and take down an opponent. These techniques leverage the opponent's momentum and body mechanics. Throws can be executed from a standing position or in response to an attack. They require skill in timing and body positioning. Practitioners practice throws to ensure they can execute them smoothly and effectively.

Grappling techniques are essential for close combat situations. These techniques involve controlling an opponent through holds, locks, and leverage. Grappling can be used to neutralize an opponent's attacks and gain a dominant position. Practitioners learn to use their body weight and positioning to control the opponent. This aspect of Kuk Sool Won is important for self-defense and restraint.

Kuk Sool Won also includes pressure point techniques. These techniques involve applying pressure to specific points on the body to cause pain or immobilize an opponent. Pressure points are sensitive areas that can disrupt the body's functions when manipulated. Practitioners must study anatomy and precision to use these techniques effectively. They provide an additional method of control in self-defense situations.

Forms, or hyung, are sequences of movements that combine various techniques. These forms help practitioners develop coordination, flow, and muscle memory. Each form has a specific pattern and purpose, teaching different aspects of movement and technique. Practicing forms allows practitioners to refine their skills and understand the principles behind the techniques.

In addition to empty-hand techniques, Kuk Sool Won includes weapons training. Practitioners learn to use traditional Korean weapons, such as swords, staffs, and spears. Weapons training enhances coordination, precision, and an understanding of martial principles. It also provides a historical and cultural context, connecting practitioners to the traditions of Korean martial arts.

Breathing techniques are incorporated into Kuk Sool Won to enhance focus and energy. Proper breathing helps regulate the body's energy and improve performance. Practitioners learn to synchronize their breathing with their movements. This coordination enhances the effectiveness of techniques and promotes mental clarity.

Another important aspect of Kuk Sool Won is meditation. Meditation helps practitioners develop a calm and focused mind. It involves techniques for relaxation, concentration, and mental discipline. Meditation is practiced regularly to enhance self-awareness and control. This mental training is essential for overall development and balance.

Kuk Sool Won emphasizes the importance of flexibility. Stretching exercises are incorporated into training to improve flexibility and prevent injuries. Flexibility enhances the range of motion and the execution of techniques. Practitioners engage in regular stretching routines to maintain and improve their flexibility.

Strength training is also a key component of Kuk Sool Won. Practitioners engage in exercises to build strength and endurance. Strength training supports the execution of powerful techniques and improves overall physical fitness. It is integrated into regular training sessions to ensure balanced development.

The principle of timing is crucial in Kuk Sool Won. Effective techniques require precise timing to execute correctly. Practitioners learn to anticipate and react to their opponent's movements. Timing involves understanding the rhythm and flow of a confrontation. It is essential for both offensive and defensive techniques.

Coordination is another vital principle in Kuk Sool Won. Practitioners must coordinate their movements to execute techniques smoothly. This involves synchronizing different parts of the body and aligning movements with intent. Coordination enhances the efficiency and effectiveness of techniques.

Balance is a foundational principle in Kuk Sool Won. Practitioners must maintain balance to move and execute techniques effectively. Balance involves proper weight distribution and body alignment. It is crucial for stability and control during combat and training.

Speed is also an important principle in Kuk Sool Won. Practitioners develop the ability to execute techniques quickly. Speed enhances the effectiveness of strikes and defenses. It involves not only physical speed but also mental quickness and reaction time.

Endurance is emphasized in Kuk Sool Won to sustain performance during training and combat. Practitioners engage in exercises to build cardiovascular endurance. This endurance supports prolonged physical activity and recovery. It is essential for maintaining effectiveness over time.

Kuk Sool Won also teaches practitioners the principle of adaptability. Practitioners learn to adjust their techniques and strategies based on the situation. Adaptability involves being flexible and open-minded. It is crucial for responding effectively to different scenarios.

The principle of precision is central to Kuk Sool Won. Techniques must be executed with accuracy to be effective. Precision involves careful attention to detail and control. Practitioners refine their movements to achieve exactness in their techniques.

Another important principle is efficiency. Techniques in Kuk Sool Won are designed to be effective with minimal effort. Efficiency involves using the body's mechanics and leverage optimally. This principle ensures that practitioners can conserve energy and achieve maximum impact.

Practitioners of Kuk Sool Won also learn the importance of posture. Proper posture supports effective movement and technique execution. Posture involves maintaining the correct alignment of the body. It enhances balance, power, and control.

Another key principle is awareness. Practitioners develop situational awareness to anticipate and respond to threats. Awareness involves being mindful of the surroundings and the opponent's actions. It is essential for effective self-defense and strategy.

Focus is crucial for the execution of techniques in Kuk Sool Won. Practitioners learn to concentrate their attention fully on their movements. Focus enhances precision, speed, and timing. It is essential for achieving the desired outcome in training and combat.

In Kuk Sool Won, the principle of relaxation is also important. Practitioners learn to relax their muscles to enhance movement fluidity. Relaxation reduces tension and improves the flow of techniques. It is essential for maintaining stamina and avoiding unnecessary strain.

In conclusion, the principles and techniques of Kuk Sool Won encompass a wide range of elements that contribute to its effectiveness as a martial art. These include proper stance, striking, blocking, joint locks, throwing, grappling, pressure points, forms, weapons training, breathing, meditation, flexibility, strength, timing, coordination, balance, speed, endurance, adaptability, precision, efficiency, posture, awareness, focus, and relaxation. Each of these elements is essential for developing a well-rounded martial artist and achieving the goals of Kuk Sool Won. Understanding and practicing these principles and techniques provide a comprehensive foundation for mastering this martial art.

Training and Practice

Training in Kuk Sool Won involves a structured and comprehensive approach to martial arts. It starts with learning the basic stances and movements, which are the foundation of all techniques. Practitioners focus on proper posture and balance, ensuring they can move efficiently and effectively. These basics are essential for building a strong foundation in Kuk Sool Won.

Students begin with simple drills to practice strikes, kicks, and blocks. These drills help develop muscle memory and coordination. Practitioners repeat these movements many times to ensure precision and accuracy. This repetitive practice is crucial for mastering the basic techniques. Each movement is performed with attention to detail, focusing on correct form and execution.

As students progress, they learn more complex techniques and combinations. These include joint locks, throws, and grappling techniques. Practitioners must understand the principles behind each technique and apply them correctly. This involves studying the mechanics of the body and how to use leverage effectively. Advanced techniques require a higher level of skill and understanding.

Practicing forms, or hyung, is a significant part of Kuk Sool Won training. Forms are sequences of movements that combine various techniques into a flowing pattern. Practitioners perform these forms to develop coordination, timing, and rhythm. Each form has a specific purpose and teaches different aspects of movement. Practicing forms helps refine techniques and build fluidity.

Kuk Sool Won training also includes sparring, where practitioners apply their techniques against a partner. Sparring helps develop timing, distance, and adaptability. It is a controlled environment where students can practice offensive and defensive techniques. Sparring sessions are supervised to ensure safety and proper technique. This practice is essential for understanding how to apply techniques in real situations.

Conditioning exercises are an important part of Kuk Sool Won training. These exercises improve strength, endurance, and flexibility. Practitioners engage in activities such as running, jumping, and calisthenics. Conditioning helps prepare the body for the physical demands of martial arts. It also reduces the risk of injury and enhances overall fitness.

Stretching is another key component of Kuk Sool Won practice. Regular stretching routines improve flexibility and range of motion. Practitioners stretch before and after training sessions to warm up the muscles and prevent injuries. Flexibility is crucial for executing techniques effectively and safely. Stretching also promotes relaxation and recovery.

Breathing exercises are integrated into Kuk Sool Won training to enhance focus and energy. Proper breathing techniques help regulate the body's energy and improve performance. Practitioners learn to synchronize their breathing with their movements. This coordination enhances the effectiveness of techniques and promotes mental clarity.

Meditation is also a part of Kuk Sool Won practice. Practitioners use meditation to develop a calm and focused mind. Meditation techniques include breathing exercises and visualization. Regular meditation helps improve concentration, reduce stress, and enhance self-awareness. It is an essential aspect of the holistic approach to training in Kuk Sool Won.

Weapons training is included in Kuk Sool Won to provide a complete martial arts education. Practitioners learn to handle traditional Korean weapons such as swords, staffs, and spears. Weapons training develops coordination, precision, and an understanding of martial principles. It also connects practitioners to the historical and cultural aspects of Kuk Sool Won.

Regular testing and evaluation are part of Kuk Sool Won training. Practitioners advance through a series of belt ranks, each representing a higher level of skill and knowledge. Testing involves demonstrating proficiency in techniques, forms, and sparring. These evaluations provide feedback and motivation for continuous improvement. They also mark significant milestones in a practitioner's journey.

Instructors play a crucial role in Kuk Sool Won training. They provide guidance, instruction, and support to students. Instructors emphasize proper technique, discipline, and respect. They create a positive and supportive learning environment. The relationship between instructors and students is built on mutual respect and trust.

Training in Kuk Sool Won requires dedication and commitment. Practitioners must attend regular classes and practice consistently. Progress may be slow at times, but perseverance is key. The journey of learning Kuk Sool Won is as important as achieving specific goals. This dedication helps develop discipline and a strong work ethic.

Kuk Sool Won training is suitable for people of all ages and abilities. Children, adults, and seniors can all benefit from the practice. Each age group has different needs and goals, and training can be adapted accordingly. Children develop focus, discipline, and self-confidence. Adults improve fitness, stress management, and self-defense skills. Seniors enhance mobility, balance, and mental sharpness.

The community aspect of Kuk Sool Won is also significant. Practitioners often form strong bonds with their fellow students and instructors. This sense of community provides encouragement and support. Training together fosters a spirit of camaraderie and mutual respect. Many schools also organize social events, seminars, and competitions to strengthen community ties.

Safety is a priority in Kuk Sool Won training. Instructors ensure that techniques are practiced correctly to prevent injuries. Protective gear is used during sparring and other high-intensity activities. Warm-up exercises and stretching are incorporated to prepare the body for training. Safety guidelines are followed to create a secure training environment.

The mental benefits of Kuk Sool Won are as important as the physical ones. Training helps improve focus, concentration, and mental clarity. The discipline and structure of Kuk Sool Won promote self-control and emotional resilience. Practitioners often find that the principles learned in training apply to other areas of life. This holistic approach fosters overall well-being.

Training in Kuk Sool Won also emphasizes the importance of setting and achieving goals. Practitioners are encouraged to set both short-term and long-term goals. This helps provide direction and motivation. Achieving these goals requires consistent effort and perseverance. Goal-setting is an important part of personal growth and development.

Kuk Sool Won practice is a journey of continuous learning and improvement. Practitioners are always seeking to refine their techniques and deepen their understanding. This mindset of lifelong learning helps maintain enthusiasm and passion for the martial art. It also ensures that practitioners are always growing and evolving.

In conclusion, training and practice in Kuk Sool Won involve a comprehensive approach that includes basic techniques, forms, sparring, conditioning, stretching, breathing exercises, meditation, and weapons training. The emphasis on dedication, community, safety, mental benefits, goal-setting, and continuous learning makes Kuk Sool Won a holistic and effective martial art. Practitioners of all ages and abilities can benefit from this well-rounded training, developing both physically and mentally through their practice.

Rank and Promotion System

Kuk Sool Won has a structured rank and promotion system designed to recognize and reward the progress of practitioners. This system motivates students to continue their training and achieve higher levels of skill and knowledge. Each rank represents a specific level of proficiency, and advancement requires dedication and effort.

The rank system begins with white belt, the starting point for all practitioners. White belt signifies a beginner with no prior experience in Kuk Sool Won. At this level, students focus on learning the basics, such as stances, strikes, and blocks. This foundational training is essential for building a solid base in martial arts.

After the white belt, practitioners progress to yellow belt. At this stage, they begin to learn more complex techniques and combinations. Yellow belt students practice joint locks, throws, and basic forms. The focus is on refining basic skills and developing a deeper understanding of Kuk Sool Won principles.

Next is the blue belt, where practitioners continue to build on their skills. Blue belt students learn more advanced forms and techniques. They practice sparring and begin to integrate weapons training into their practice. This level requires increased coordination and control. Students are encouraged to develop their strength and flexibility further.

The red belt follows the blue belt, marking a significant advancement in skill and knowledge. Red belt practitioners focus on mastering complex techniques and forms. They also deepen their understanding of the principles behind each movement. This level involves more intensive training and higher expectations for performance.

After red belt, students achieve brown belt. Brown belt signifies an advanced level of proficiency in Kuk Sool Won. Practitioners at this level are skilled in a wide range of techniques, including advanced joint locks, throws, and pressure points. They are also proficient in various weapons. Brown belt students are expected to demonstrate a high level of precision and control.

Black belt is the next significant milestone in Kuk Sool Won. Earning a black belt represents a deep commitment to the martial art and a high level of skill and knowledge. Black belt practitioners have mastered the foundational techniques and principles of Kuk Sool Won. They continue to refine their skills and expand their understanding. Achieving a black belt requires years of dedicated practice and training.

Within the black belt ranks, there are several degrees of advancement. First-degree black belts continue to develop their skills and knowledge. They take on more responsibility within the Kuk Sool Won community, often assisting with instruction and mentoring lower-rank students. Each subsequent degree represents further mastery and contribution to the martial art.

Promotion within the black belt ranks involves rigorous testing and evaluation. Practitioners must demonstrate their proficiency in techniques, forms, sparring, and weapons. They are also evaluated on their understanding of Kuk Sool Won principles and philosophy. The promotion process is challenging and requires significant preparation and effort.

In addition to the technical skills, the rank and promotion system emphasizes the development of character and values. Practitioners are expected to embody the principles of respect, humility, self-discipline, and integrity. These qualities are essential for advancing in rank and becoming a well-rounded martial artist.

Testing for promotion typically involves a formal evaluation by senior instructors. Practitioners perform their techniques and forms in front of a panel of judges. They may also participate in sparring sessions and demonstrate their knowledge of Kuk Sool Won history and philosophy. This comprehensive assessment ensures that practitioners meet the standards for their new rank.

The promotion system also includes a ceremony to recognize the achievements of practitioners. These ceremonies are an important part of the Kuk Sool Won tradition. They provide an opportunity to celebrate the hard work and dedication of students. Families and friends often attend to show their support and encouragement.

Instructors play a crucial role in guiding students through the rank and promotion process. They provide instruction, feedback, and encouragement. Instructors help students set goals and develop a plan to achieve them. Their support is essential for the progress and success of practitioners.

Kuk Sool Won schools often have a structured curriculum to ensure consistency in training. This curriculum outlines the techniques, forms, and knowledge required for each rank. Practitioners follow this curriculum to prepare for promotions. It provides a clear path for progression and ensures that all students receive a comprehensive education in Kuk Sool Won.

The rank and promotion system also fosters a sense of community and camaraderie. Practitioners support each other in their training and celebrate each other's achievements. This sense of community is important for maintaining motivation and enthusiasm. It creates a positive and supportive environment for learning and growth.

Achieving higher ranks in Kuk Sool Won is not just about technical proficiency. It also involves personal growth and development. Practitioners learn to set and achieve goals, overcome challenges, and develop resilience. The journey through the ranks is a path of continuous improvement and self-discovery.

The rank and promotion system is designed to be challenging but attainable. It encourages practitioners to push their limits and strive for excellence. Each new rank is a milestone that represents significant progress and achievement. This system helps practitioners stay motivated and engaged in their training.

In conclusion, the rank and promotion system in Kuk Sool Won is a structured and comprehensive process that recognizes and rewards the progress of practitioners. It begins with the white belt and advances through various colored belts to the black belt and its degrees. This system emphasizes technical proficiency, character development, and personal growth. It provides a clear path for advancement and fosters a supportive and motivating community. Understanding and participating in this system is essential for achieving success in Kuk Sool Won.

Forms and Patterns (Hyung)

Forms, also known as hyung, are a crucial aspect of Kuk Sool Won. They consist of prearranged sequences of movements that incorporate various techniques. Practitioners perform these sequences to develop coordination, balance, and muscle memory. Each form has a specific purpose and teaches different aspects of martial arts.

Hyung practice begins with learning basic forms. These forms introduce fundamental movements and techniques. Practitioners focus on executing each movement precisely and fluidly. Basic forms help build a strong foundation for more advanced techniques. They are repeated regularly to reinforce muscle memory and improve accuracy.

As practitioners progress, they learn more complex forms. These advanced forms incorporate a wider range of techniques, including strikes, blocks, and kicks. Practitioners must pay attention to details such as timing, posture, and direction. Advanced forms challenge practitioners to refine their skills and increase their understanding of movement.

Hyung practice also includes weapon forms. These forms involve traditional Korean weapons such as swords, staffs, and spears. Practitioners learn to handle these weapons with precision and control. Weapon forms teach coordination and enhance understanding of martial principles. They also connect practitioners to the historical and cultural aspects of Kuk Sool Won.

Each form in Kuk Sool Won has a specific pattern and sequence. Practitioners must memorize these sequences and perform them accurately. The patterns are designed to simulate combat scenarios, allowing practitioners to practice techniques in a structured manner. Memorizing and performing forms requires concentration and mental discipline.

Forms help develop physical attributes such as strength, flexibility, and endurance. The repeated practice of movements builds muscle strength and improves joint flexibility. Performing forms also requires sustained effort, which enhances cardiovascular endurance. These physical benefits contribute to overall fitness and well-being.

Hyung practice also enhances mental attributes. Practitioners must maintain focus and concentration to perform forms correctly. This mental discipline helps improve attention to detail and the ability to stay present in the moment. The practice of forms also promotes mental clarity and reduces stress.

Forms in Kuk Sool Won are performed at different speeds and intensities. Practitioners may perform forms slowly to focus on precision and control. They may also perform forms at a faster pace to simulate real combat conditions. Varying the speed and intensity helps practitioners develop adaptability and versatility in their techniques.

Each form has specific applications that relate to self-defense scenarios. Practitioners learn to understand the purpose behind each movement and how it can be applied in real situations. This practical understanding is essential for effective self-defense. It also deepens the practitioner's appreciation of the form's complexity and purpose.

Forms are often performed in a group setting, allowing practitioners to practice together. Group practice helps build a sense of camaraderie and mutual support. Practitioners can observe and learn from each other, enhancing their own performance. Group practice also fosters a sense of community and shared purpose.

Hyung practice includes regular feedback and evaluation from instructors. Instructors provide guidance on improving technique and form. They help practitioners identify areas for improvement and set goals for progress. This feedback is crucial for continuous improvement and mastery of forms.

Forms are an essential part of Kuk Sool Won testing and promotion. Practitioners must demonstrate their proficiency in forms to advance to higher ranks. The ability to perform forms accurately and confidently is a key criterion for promotion. This requirement ensures that practitioners have a thorough understanding of the techniques and principles of Kuk Sool Won.

Practicing forms also has a meditative aspect. The repetitive and structured nature of forms allows practitioners to enter a focused and relaxed state. This meditative practice helps reduce stress and improve mental well-being. It also enhances the practitioner's connection to their body and movements.

Forms are a way to preserve and transmit the knowledge and traditions of Kuk Sool Won. Each form embodies the techniques and principles developed over centuries. By practicing forms, practitioners connect with the history and lineage of Kuk Sool Won. This preservation of tradition is an important aspect of the martial art.

The practice of forms also promotes discipline and perseverance. Learning and mastering forms requires consistent practice and dedication. Practitioners must overcome challenges and persist in their training. This discipline and perseverance are valuable traits that extend beyond martial arts practice.

Forms provide a structured way to measure progress and improvement. Practitioners can track their development by comparing their performance of forms over time. As they refine their techniques and increase their understanding, their forms become more fluid and precise. This measurable progress is motivating and rewarding.

Hyung practice also includes public demonstrations and competitions. Practitioners perform forms in front of an audience or judges, showcasing their skills and proficiency. These events provide an opportunity to test and demonstrate what they have learned. Public performance helps build confidence and poise.

Forms are practiced at all levels of Kuk Sool Won, from beginners to advanced practitioners. Each level introduces new forms that increase in complexity. This progression ensures that practitioners are constantly challenged and continue to develop their skills. The structured curriculum of forms provides a clear path for advancement.

In conclusion, forms, or hyung, are a fundamental component of Kuk Sool Won. They involve prearranged sequences of movements that teach coordination, balance, and muscle memory. Forms range from basic to advanced, incorporating a variety of techniques and weapons. Practicing forms enhances both physical and mental attributes, including strength, flexibility, concentration, and mental clarity. Forms also provide a way to understand and apply self-defense techniques. They foster discipline, perseverance, and a connection to the history and traditions of Kuk Sool Won. Forms are essential for measuring progress, achieving promotions, and participating in demonstrations and competitions. Understanding and mastering forms is crucial for the overall development of a Kuk Sool Won practitioner.

Self-Defense Techniques

Self-defense techniques in Kuk Sool Won are designed to protect oneself from various threats. These techniques incorporate a mix of strikes, blocks, joint locks, throws, and pressure points. Practitioners learn to respond effectively to different types of attacks, emphasizing control and precision.

Striking techniques are fundamental for self-defense. Practitioners learn to use their hands, feet, elbows, and knees to deliver powerful strikes. These strikes aim at vital points on the attacker's body to incapacitate them quickly. Practicing strikes involves developing speed, power, and accuracy. This training ensures that practitioners can effectively defend themselves in dangerous situations.

Blocking techniques are equally essential. Practitioners learn to deflect or stop attacks using their arms and legs. Blocks can redirect the force of an attack or create openings for counterattacks. Effective blocking requires good timing and coordination. Practitioners practice different types of blocks to handle various attacks, such as punches, kicks, and weapon strikes.

Joint locks are another crucial self-defense technique. These involve manipulating the attacker's joints to cause pain and control their movements. Practitioners apply joint locks to the wrists, elbows, shoulders, and other joints. Joint locks are effective for subduing an attacker without causing permanent injury. Learning these techniques requires precision and an understanding of human anatomy.

Throwing techniques allow practitioners to unbalance and take down an attacker. These techniques use leverage and the attacker's momentum to execute the throw. Practitioners learn to perform throws from various positions, both standing and in response to attacks. Throws help create distance and gain control over the attacker. Practicing throws develops timing, balance, and body mechanics.

Grappling techniques are used for close-range self-defense. Practitioners learn to control and neutralize an attacker through holds and locks. Grappling involves using body weight and positioning to dominate the attacker. These techniques are useful when an attacker grabs or restrains the practitioner. Training in grappling enhances strength, control, and situational awareness.

Pressure point techniques target sensitive areas on the attacker's body. Applying pressure to these points can cause pain, immobilization, or unconsciousness. Practitioners learn to identify and use pressure points effectively. These techniques require precise knowledge of anatomy and careful application.

Pressure points add another layer of effectiveness to self-defense.

Practitioners also learn defensive techniques against weapon attacks. These techniques involve disarming the attacker and neutralizing the threat. Practitioners practice defending against knives, sticks, and other weapons. Defensive strategies include evasion, blocks, and counters. Training with weapons enhances reflexes and quick decision-making.

Situational awareness is a key aspect of self-defense. Practitioners are taught to be aware of their surroundings and potential threats. This awareness helps in recognizing and avoiding dangerous situations. Practicing situational awareness involves observing the environment and identifying escape routes. It is essential for preventing attacks and staying safe.

Self-defense training in Kuk Sool Won also includes scenario-based practice. Practitioners simulate real-life situations to apply their techniques under realistic conditions. These scenarios help develop quick thinking and adaptability. Practicing in different scenarios prepares practitioners for various threats they might encounter.

Escape techniques are crucial for self-defense. Practitioners learn how to break free from grabs and holds. These techniques involve using leverage and movement to escape. Practicing escape techniques ensures that practitioners can free themselves from restraints quickly. This ability is vital for protecting oneself in close encounters.

Kuk Sool Won emphasizes the importance of controlling the level of force used in self-defense. Practitioners are taught to use the minimum force necessary to neutralize the threat. This principle ensures that self-defense actions are appropriate and do not cause unnecessary harm. Training includes understanding when to escalate or de-escalate the level of force.

Defensive techniques also incorporate footwork and movement. Practitioners learn to move effectively to avoid attacks and create advantageous positions. Good footwork helps maintain balance and control during self-defense situations. Practicing movement enhances agility and the ability to respond quickly to attacks.

Practitioners are trained to use their voice in self-defense. Shouting can startle an attacker and attract attention. Using the voice assertively can also deter potential threats. Practicing vocal techniques helps practitioners use their voice effectively in dangerous situations. This strategy adds an extra layer of protection.

Self-defense training in Kuk Sool Won includes mental preparation. Practitioners learn to stay calm and focused during stressful situations. Mental discipline helps in making quick and effective decisions. Techniques such as visualization and controlled breathing are used to enhance mental readiness. This mental training is crucial for effective self-defense.

Instructors play a vital role in teaching self-defense techniques. They provide guidance, feedback, and support to practitioners. Instructors ensure that techniques are practiced correctly and safely. Their experience and knowledge help students develop confidence in their self-defense abilities. The relationship between instructors and students is based on trust and respect.

Regular practice is essential for mastering self-defense techniques. Practitioners must consistently train to maintain and improve their skills. Repetition helps in developing muscle memory and reflexes. Regular practice also builds confidence and readiness. Commitment to practice is necessary for effective self-defense.

The principles of self-defense in Kuk Sool Won extend beyond physical techniques. Practitioners are taught to de-escalate situations and avoid conflict when possible. This approach promotes safety and responsibility. Understanding the legal and ethical implications of self-defense is also emphasized. Practitioners learn to act within the bounds of the law and with respect for others.

Self-defense training benefits practitioners in many ways. It improves physical fitness, including strength, flexibility, and endurance. It also enhances mental attributes such as confidence, focus, and resilience. Learning self-defense empowers practitioners and increases their sense of security. The skills and principles learned in training are applicable in many aspects of life.

Training also fosters a sense of community among practitioners. They support and learn from each other during practice. This camaraderie provides encouragement and motivation. The shared goal of mastering self-defense techniques creates a strong bond. This sense of community enhances the overall training experience.

In conclusion, self-defense techniques in Kuk Sool Won encompass a wide range of methods to protect oneself from threats. These include striking, blocking, joint locks, throws, grappling, pressure points, and weapon defenses. Practitioners also focus on situational awareness, escape techniques, and appropriate use of force. Mental preparation, regular practice, and guidance from instructors are essential. The principles of self-defense extend beyond physical skills to include de-escalation and legal considerations. Training in self-defense improves physical fitness, mental resilience, and overall confidence. The supportive community further enhances the effectiveness and enjoyment of training in Kuk Sool Won.

Weapon Training

Weapon training is an integral part of Kuk Sool Won, providing practitioners with the skills to handle traditional Korean weapons. This training enhances coordination, precision, and understanding of martial principles. Weapons training also connects practitioners to the historical and cultural heritage of Korean martial arts.

One of the primary weapons in Kuk Sool Won is the sword. Sword training begins with learning basic handling and movements. Practitioners practice drawing and sheathing the sword smoothly. They learn basic strikes, blocks, and stances. Proper grip and posture are emphasized to ensure control and effectiveness.

Staff training is another fundamental aspect. The staff, a long wooden weapon, requires different techniques from the sword. Practitioners learn to wield the staff with both hands, performing strikes, blocks, and spins. Staff training improves strength and coordination. It also teaches practitioners to use leverage and momentum.

Spear training involves using a long weapon with a pointed end. Practitioners learn thrusting, sweeping, and blocking techniques. The spear's length provides an advantage in maintaining distance from an opponent. Training with the spear enhances precision and timing. Practitioners must learn to control the spear's reach and speed.

Knife training focuses on using smaller, handheld weapons. Practitioners learn to handle knives safely and effectively. Techniques include slashing, stabbing, and parrying. Knife training requires quick reflexes and agility. It also teaches practitioners to defend against knife attacks. Proper handling is crucial to avoid injury.

Other traditional weapons include the short stick and the cane. Short stick training involves strikes, blocks, and joint locks. The cane, similar in use to the staff, provides a practical self-defense tool. Practitioners learn to use these weapons in close combat situations. Training with these weapons develops versatility.

Weapons training includes both offensive and defensive techniques. Practitioners learn to strike with precision and power. They also practice blocking and deflecting attacks. Defensive techniques involve using the weapon to protect oneself and create openings for counterattacks. This balanced approach ensures comprehensive skill development.

Kuk Sool Won weapons training incorporates forms, or hyung. These forms are sequences of movements performed with weapons. Practitioners learn specific forms for each weapon, combining strikes, blocks, and stances. Practicing forms helps develop muscle memory and fluidity. It also enhances understanding of the weapon's capabilities.

Sparring with weapons is a controlled practice method. Practitioners engage in mock combat to apply their techniques. Sparring improves timing, distance management, and adaptability. Safety gear and supervision are essential during weapon sparring. This practice simulates real combat scenarios.

Weapon training also includes drills to enhance specific skills. Practitioners perform repetitive movements to improve speed, accuracy, and coordination. Drills help in refining techniques and building confidence. Consistent practice of drills is crucial for mastering weapon skills.

Instructors play a vital role in weapon training. They provide guidance on proper techniques and safety. Instructors ensure that practitioners handle weapons correctly and effectively. Their expertise helps students progress and avoid injuries. The relationship between instructor and student is built on respect and trust.

Weapons training requires discipline and focus. Practitioners must pay attention to detail and execute movements precisely. This discipline translates to other areas of martial arts and daily life. The focus developed in weapon training enhances overall mental clarity.

Training with weapons also involves understanding the historical context. Each weapon has a unique history and significance. Practitioners learn about the origins and traditional uses of the weapons. This knowledge enriches the training experience and connects practitioners to Korean martial heritage.

Proper maintenance of weapons is an important aspect of training. Practitioners learn to care for their weapons, ensuring they remain in good condition. Maintenance includes cleaning, sharpening, and storing weapons correctly. This responsibility teaches respect for the tools of martial arts.

Weapons training is suitable for practitioners of all levels. Beginners start with basic techniques and progress to more advanced skills. Advanced practitioners refine their techniques and learn complex forms. The structured progression ensures continuous development.

Practicing with weapons enhances physical fitness. Weapon training improves strength, flexibility, and endurance. The physical demands of handling weapons provide a comprehensive workout. Regular practice contributes to overall health and well-being.

Mental benefits are also significant in weapons training. Practitioners develop concentration, patience, and resilience. The challenges of learning and mastering weapon techniques foster mental toughness. This mental discipline is valuable both in martial arts and in everyday life.

Weapon training promotes a sense of accomplishment and confidence. As practitioners master new techniques and forms, they build self-assurance. This confidence extends to other areas of life, enhancing personal growth. Achieving proficiency in weapons training is a rewarding experience.

The community aspect of weapons training is also important. Practitioners often train together, supporting and motivating each other. This camaraderie creates a positive and encouraging training environment. Shared goals and experiences build strong bonds among practitioners.

Weapons training in Kuk Sool Won is recognized in demonstrations and competitions. Practitioners showcase their skills in public performances. These events provide an opportunity to demonstrate proficiency and share the art with others. Competitions offer a platform to test skills against peers.

Training with weapons also involves learning the ethical use of these tools. Practitioners are taught to use weapons responsibly and only for self-defense. The principles of respect and integrity guide the use of martial arts skills. This ethical foundation is crucial for maintaining the integrity of the art.

In conclusion, weapon training in Kuk Sool Won encompasses a comprehensive and structured approach. Practitioners learn to handle traditional Korean weapons such as swords, staffs, spears, knives, and more. Training includes forms, drills, sparring, and historical knowledge. Instructors provide guidance and ensure safety. Discipline, focus, and respect are key components. Weapon training enhances physical and mental attributes, builds confidence, and fosters a sense of community. Understanding the ethical use of weapons is essential.

Overall, weapon training enriches the martial arts experience and connects practitioners to the rich heritage of Kuk Sool Won.

Healing Arts

The healing arts in Kuk Sool Won are an essential aspect of its holistic approach. These practices focus on maintaining and improving health, preventing injuries, and enhancing recovery. The integration of healing arts ensures that practitioners not only learn martial techniques but also understand how to care for their bodies.

One of the primary components of healing arts in Kuk Sool Won is acupressure. Acupressure involves applying pressure to specific points on the body to relieve pain and promote healing. These points, known as acupoints, are connected by pathways called meridians. Practitioners learn to identify and stimulate these points to improve energy flow and alleviate discomfort.

Massage therapy is another significant element. It involves manipulating the muscles and tissues to enhance circulation, reduce tension, and promote relaxation. Different techniques are used to address various issues, such as muscle stiffness, stress, and fatigue. Regular massage helps maintain muscle health and prevents injuries.

Herbal medicine plays a vital role in the healing arts of Kuk Sool Won. Practitioners use natural herbs to treat and prevent ailments. Herbal remedies can address a wide range of conditions, from digestive issues to respiratory problems. Understanding the properties and uses of different herbs is essential for effective treatment.

Breathing exercises are also emphasized in the healing arts. Proper breathing techniques help regulate the body's energy and promote relaxation. These exercises can improve lung capacity, reduce stress, and enhance overall well-being. Practicing controlled breathing is an integral part of maintaining health in Kuk Sool Won.

Meditation is another crucial practice. It involves focusing the mind and achieving a state of calmness and clarity. Meditation techniques include mindfulness, visualization, and controlled breathing. Regular meditation helps reduce stress, improve mental focus, and enhance emotional stability. It is a key component of the holistic approach to health.

Stretching exercises are essential for maintaining flexibility and preventing injuries. Practitioners engage in regular stretching routines to keep their muscles and joints supple. Stretching helps improve the range of motion, reduce muscle stiffness, and enhance overall physical performance. It is an important part of the healing arts in Kuk Sool Won.

Diet and nutrition are also important in the healing arts. Practitioners are encouraged to maintain a balanced and healthy diet. Proper nutrition supports overall health, energy levels, and recovery. Understanding the impact of different foods on the body is crucial for maintaining optimal health.

Hydration is another key aspect. Drinking adequate amounts of water is essential for maintaining bodily functions and overall health. Proper hydration supports energy levels, digestion, and recovery. Practitioners are taught the importance of staying hydrated, especially during intense training sessions.

Injury prevention is a significant focus in the healing arts. Practitioners learn techniques and strategies to avoid injuries during training and daily activities. This includes proper warm-up routines, correct technique execution, and understanding body mechanics. Preventing injuries is crucial for maintaining long-term health and performance.

Recovery techniques are also a vital part of the healing arts. These techniques help practitioners recover quickly from training sessions and injuries. Methods include rest, proper nutrition, hydration, and specific recovery exercises. Effective recovery practices ensure that practitioners can maintain consistent training without setbacks.

Mental health is also addressed in the healing arts. Practices such as meditation, breathing exercises, and stress management techniques help maintain mental well-being. Practitioners learn to balance their physical and mental health for overall wellness. Maintaining mental health is essential for achieving peak performance and well-being.

Energy work, such as Qi Gong, is another component of the healing arts. These practices involve movements and exercises designed to cultivate and balance the body's energy. Qi Gong can improve vitality, reduce stress, and enhance overall health. Understanding and practicing energy work is part of the holistic approach to healing.

Proper sleep is also emphasized. Getting adequate rest is crucial for recovery and overall health. Practitioners are encouraged to develop good sleep habits and understand the importance of rest. Proper sleep supports physical performance, mental clarity, and emotional stability.

Emotional health is another focus in the healing arts. Techniques such as mindfulness and meditation help manage emotions and reduce stress. Practitioners learn to maintain emotional balance and resilience. Emotional health is important for overall well-being and effective martial arts practice.

Self-care practices are encouraged to maintain health and well-being. This includes regular exercise, balanced nutrition, proper hydration, and stress management. Practitioners are taught to prioritize self-care and understand its importance. Effective self-care supports long-term health and performance.

Understanding anatomy and physiology is part of the healing arts education. Practitioners learn about the body's structure and functions. This knowledge helps them understand how to prevent injuries and promote healing. It is essential for applying techniques such as acupressure and massage effectively.

Regular check-ups and health monitoring are encouraged. Practitioners are taught to be proactive about their health. Regular health assessments help identify potential issues early and address them promptly. This proactive approach supports long-term health and well-being.

Integrating the healing arts with martial arts practice creates a balanced approach. Practitioners learn to care for their bodies while developing martial skills. This integration ensures that they can train effectively and maintain their health. The holistic approach enhances overall well-being and martial arts performance.

The healing arts also foster a sense of community. Practitioners often share knowledge and support each other in maintaining health. This sense of community encourages mutual care and well-being. It creates a supportive environment for learning and growth.

Instructors play a crucial role in teaching the healing arts. They provide guidance, instruction, and support to practitioners. Instructors ensure that techniques are practiced correctly and safely. Their knowledge and experience are essential for effective healing arts practice.

The healing arts in Kuk Sool Won are suitable for practitioners of all ages and abilities. Each individual can benefit from these practices, regardless of their martial arts experience. The healing arts promote overall health and well-being. They are an integral part of the comprehensive approach to training in Kuk Sool Won.

In conclusion, the healing arts in Kuk Sool Won encompass a wide range of practices designed to maintain and improve health. These include acupressure, massage therapy, herbal medicine, breathing exercises, meditation, stretching, diet, hydration, injury prevention, recovery techniques, mental health practices, energy work, proper sleep, emotional health, self-care, anatomy knowledge, regular check-ups, and a sense of community. Instructors provide essential guidance and support. The healing arts create a balanced approach to martial arts training, enhancing overall well-being and performance. Understanding and practicing these arts is crucial for a holistic martial arts experience.

Modern Applications and Adaptations

Kuk Sool Won has evolved to include modern applications and adaptations while retaining its traditional roots. This evolution ensures that the martial art remains relevant and effective in contemporary contexts. Practitioners learn to apply traditional techniques in modern scenarios, enhancing their versatility and practicality.

One significant adaptation is the incorporation of modern self-defense strategies. Practitioners are taught to handle current threats such as muggings, assaults, and other street crimes. Techniques are adjusted to address these situations effectively. This includes awareness of surroundings, quick decision-making, and appropriate responses to various threats.

The use of modern training equipment is another adaptation. Practitioners utilize equipment such as punching bags, focus mitts, and padded suits. These tools enhance training by allowing practitioners to practice strikes and techniques with full force. Modern equipment helps improve accuracy, power, and safety during practice.

Fitness training has also been integrated into Kuk Sool Won. Modern fitness principles are applied to improve strength, endurance, and flexibility. Practitioners engage in cardio workouts, strength training, and functional exercises. This integration ensures that practitioners are physically fit and capable of performing techniques effectively.

Technological advancements have influenced training methods. Practitioners use video analysis to review and improve their techniques. Recording and playback allow for detailed examination of movements and corrections. This use of technology enhances learning and helps practitioners achieve higher levels of precision.

Kuk Sool Won schools often incorporate self-defense seminars and workshops. These sessions address specific modern threats such as personal safety, workplace violence, and travel security. Participants learn practical techniques and strategies to protect themselves in various environments. These seminars make the martial art accessible and applicable to a wider audience.

Modern teaching methods have also been adopted. Instructors use a variety of teaching tools and techniques to cater to different learning styles. This includes visual aids, interactive demonstrations, and hands-on practice. Modern pedagogy ensures that all students can effectively learn and apply Kuk Sool Won techniques.

Women's self-defense has become a focus in Kuk Sool Won. Special programs and classes are designed to address the unique threats faced by women. Techniques and strategies are tailored to empower women and build confidence. These programs create a supportive environment for women to learn and practice self-defense.

The integration of mental health practices is another modern adaptation. Kuk Sool Won incorporates mindfulness, stress management, and mental resilience training. Practitioners learn techniques to manage stress and maintain mental clarity. This holistic approach supports overall well-being and enhances martial arts performance.

Community engagement is emphasized in modern Kuk Sool Won practice. Schools often participate in community events, demonstrations, and outreach programs. These activities promote martial arts and build community connections. Engaging with the community helps spread the benefits of Kuk Sool Won and attract new practitioners.

Modern Kuk Sool Won training includes first aid and emergency response skills. Practitioners learn basic first aid techniques and how to respond to injuries. This knowledge is crucial for ensuring safety during training and in everyday life. Understanding first aid enhances the overall safety and preparedness of practitioners.

The adaptation of Kuk Sool Won for children and youth is significant. Programs are tailored to suit younger practitioners, focusing on discipline, confidence, and physical fitness. Techniques are simplified and taught in a fun, engaging manner. These programs help children develop important life skills through martial arts.

Senior practitioners also benefit from adapted training. Kuk Sool Won offers programs that focus on mobility, balance, and gentle exercise. Techniques are modified to suit the needs of older adults. These programs promote health, independence, and quality of life for senior practitioners.

Corporate training programs are another modern application. Kuk Sool Won offers workshops and seminars for businesses and organizations. These programs focus on team building, stress management, and personal safety. Corporate training helps employees develop valuable skills and improve workplace dynamics.

The use of online resources and training has increased. Practitioners can access instructional videos, virtual classes, and forums. Online platforms allow for continued learning and practice, even outside the training hall. This flexibility makes Kuk Sool Won accessible to a broader audience.

Kuk Sool Won competitions have evolved to include modern formats. Tournaments and competitions now feature a variety of events, including forms, sparring, and weapons demonstrations. These events provide opportunities for practitioners to showcase their skills and compete. Modern competitions help maintain interest and excitement in the martial art.

The integration of cross-training with other martial arts is another adaptation. Practitioners are encouraged to explore and incorporate techniques from other disciplines. This cross-training enhances their versatility and understanding of martial arts. It also promotes a more comprehensive approach to self-defense and combat.

Environmental awareness and sustainability are incorporated into modern practice. Schools promote eco-friendly practices and mindfulness of environmental impact. This includes reducing waste, conserving resources, and promoting sustainability. Environmental awareness aligns with the holistic principles of Kuk Sool Won.

Modern Kuk Sool Won also addresses cultural sensitivity and inclusivity. Schools create inclusive environments that welcome practitioners from diverse backgrounds. Cultural sensitivity training ensures that all practitioners feel respected and valued. This inclusivity enriches the martial arts community and promotes mutual respect.

Adaptation to modern lifestyles is a key focus. Kuk Sool Won training schedules are designed to accommodate busy lives. Classes are offered at various times to suit different schedules. This flexibility ensures that practitioners can integrate martial arts training into their daily routines.

In conclusion, modern applications and adaptations of Kuk Sool Won ensure its relevance and effectiveness. These adaptations include modern self-defense strategies, training equipment, fitness principles, technological advancements, self-defense seminars, modern teaching methods, women's self-defense, mental health practices, community engagement, first aid training, programs for children and seniors, corporate training, online resources, modern competitions, cross-training, environmental awareness, cultural sensitivity, and flexible training schedules. These adaptations enhance the overall practice of Kuk Sool Won, making it accessible and applicable to contemporary life. Practitioners benefit from a comprehensive and holistic approach to martial arts that addresses modern needs and challenges. Understanding and embracing these modern adaptations ensures that Kuk Sool Won continues to thrive and evolve in the modern world.

Kuk Sool Won in Popular Culture

Kuk Sool Won has made its mark in popular culture through various media, showcasing its unique blend of martial arts techniques and philosophy. This exposure has helped spread awareness of the martial art and attract new practitioners worldwide. The representation of Kuk Sool Won in films, television shows, and other media highlights its dynamic techniques and rich heritage.

Films featuring Kuk Sool Won demonstrate the art's versatility and effectiveness. Action movies often incorporate Kuk Sool Won techniques in fight scenes, showcasing its striking, joint locks, and throws. These films highlight the martial art's practical application in combat scenarios. The choreography of these scenes emphasizes the fluidity and precision of Kuk Sool Won movements, capturing the audience's attention.

Television shows have also played a significant role in popularizing Kuk Sool Won. Martial arts-themed series often include characters who practice Kuk Sool Won, demonstrating techniques and forms. These shows provide a platform for showcasing the art's principles and methods. The depiction of Kuk Sool Won in television helps educate viewers about its philosophy and applications, increasing interest in the martial art.

Documentaries focusing on martial arts have featured Kuk Sool Won, providing an in-depth look at its history and practices. These documentaries explore the origins, development, and cultural significance of Kuk Sool Won. They include interviews with practitioners and instructors, offering insights into their experiences and the benefits of training. This format allows for a comprehensive understanding of the martial art.

Kuk Sool Won practitioners have participated in martial arts competitions and demonstrations, further raising its profile. Public demonstrations at events and festivals showcase the art's techniques and forms. These performances highlight the skill and dedication of practitioners, captivating audiences. Competitions provide a platform for practitioners to test their abilities and gain recognition, promoting the martial art.

The inclusion of Kuk Sool Won in video games has also contributed to its popularity. Martial arts video games often feature characters that use Kuk Sool Won techniques. Players can engage with the martial art virtually, learning about its movements and applications. This interactive format makes Kuk Sool Won accessible to a younger audience, sparking interest in real-life practice.

Books and publications about Kuk Sool Won have provided valuable resources for practitioners and enthusiasts. Instructional books detail techniques, forms, and the philosophy behind the martial art. Biographies of prominent Kuk Sool Won masters offer inspirational stories and insights into their journeys. These publications serve as educational tools and sources of inspiration for readers.

Social media platforms have become a powerful tool for promoting Kuk Sool Won. Practitioners and schools share videos, photos, and articles about their training and experiences. These posts reach a global audience, connecting practitioners and attracting new students. Social media allows for real-time updates and interactions, fostering a sense of community among Kuk Sool Won enthusiasts.

Kuk Sool Won has been featured in various magazines and online articles. Martial arts magazines often include articles about Kuk Sool Won techniques, training methods, and events. Online platforms provide news, interviews, and tutorials related to the martial art. This coverage helps keep practitioners informed and engaged with the broader Kuk Sool Won community.

The influence of Kuk Sool Won extends to the entertainment industry, with some celebrities and public figures practicing the martial art. Their involvement brings additional attention and credibility to Kuk Sool Won. Public endorsements by well-known individuals help raise awareness and attract a diverse audience to the martial art.

Workshops and seminars led by Kuk Sool Won masters have been organized worldwide. These events offer intensive training sessions and opportunities to learn from experienced instructors. Workshops and seminars provide a deeper understanding of techniques and principles, enhancing the skills of participants. They also foster a sense of camaraderie among practitioners from different regions.

Kuk Sool Won has been integrated into educational programs in some schools and universities. Martial arts classes and clubs offer students the chance to learn Kuk Sool Won as part of their physical education. This integration promotes physical fitness, discipline, and cultural awareness. Educational institutions provide a structured environment for learning and practicing the martial art.

Community outreach programs organized by Kuk Sool Won schools contribute to its popularity. These programs offer free or low-cost classes to underserved communities. Outreach initiatives promote the benefits of martial arts training, such as self-discipline, confidence, and physical fitness. Community involvement helps build positive relationships and expand the reach of Kuk Sool Won.

Kuk Sool Won's presence in pop culture has led to collaborations with other martial arts and fitness disciplines. Joint events and training sessions with different martial arts schools foster mutual learning and respect. These collaborations broaden the horizons of practitioners and introduce Kuk Sool Won to new audiences. They also highlight the universal appeal of martial arts.

The martial art's representation in popular culture has also influenced fashion and merchandise. Kuk Sool Won-themed clothing, accessories, and equipment are available for enthusiasts. Branded merchandise promotes the martial art and allows practitioners to express their affiliation. The availability of themed products enhances the visibility of Kuk Sool Won.

The portrayal of Kuk Sool Won in popular culture often emphasizes its philosophical foundations. Films, shows, and books highlight the importance of respect, discipline, and perseverance. These values resonate with audiences and underscore the holistic approach of Kuk Sool Won. The emphasis on philosophy adds depth to the martial art's representation.

Kuk Sool Won's inclusion in popular culture has contributed to its global spread. Practitioners and schools can be found in many countries, fostering a diverse and international community. The martial art's adaptability and appeal transcend cultural and geographical boundaries. Its global presence enriches the practice and promotes cultural exchange.

The influence of Kuk Sool Won in popular culture continues to grow. New media representations, events, and collaborations keep the martial art in the public eye. The ongoing evolution of its portrayal ensures that Kuk Sool Won remains relevant and engaging. Continuous promotion and adaptation help sustain its popularity.

In conclusion, Kuk Sool Won's presence in popular culture encompasses films, television, documentaries, competitions, video games, books, social media, magazines, celebrity endorsements, workshops, educational programs, community outreach, collaborations, merchandise, philosophical emphasis, global spread, and ongoing influence. These representations showcase the martial art's techniques, philosophy, and cultural heritage. They attract new practitioners, promote awareness, and enhance the visibility of Kuk Sool Won. The integration of Kuk Sool Won into popular culture highlights its versatility and adaptability, ensuring its continued relevance and growth. Understanding and appreciating these cultural representations enrich the practice and experience of Kuk Sool Won for practitioners and enthusiasts alike.

Conclusion

Kuk Sool Won is a comprehensive martial art that integrates various techniques and principles from traditional Korean martial arts. It emphasizes a holistic approach, combining physical training with mental and spiritual development. Practitioners learn a wide range of techniques, including strikes, blocks, joint locks, throws, and weapons training. Each technique is designed to improve physical fitness, coordination, and self-defense skills.

The philosophical foundations of Kuk Sool Won are integral to its practice. These principles include respect, humility, self-discipline, perseverance, integrity, balance, loyalty, courage, compassion, patience, harmony, focus, gratitude, mindfulness, adaptability, responsibility, unity, and honor. Practitioners are encouraged to embody these values in their training and daily lives. The philosophy of Kuk Sool Won promotes personal growth and development.

Training in Kuk Sool Won involves a structured curriculum that progresses from basic to advanced techniques. Beginners start with foundational skills such as stances and basic strikes. As they advance, they learn more complex techniques and forms. Regular practice and dedication are essential for mastering these skills. Practitioners also engage in sparring, conditioning, and stretching exercises to improve overall fitness and performance.

The rank and promotion system in Kuk Sool Won provides a clear path for advancement. Practitioners start at white belt and progress through various colored belts to achieve black belt status. Each rank represents a higher level of proficiency and knowledge. Testing for promotion involves demonstrating techniques, forms, and sparring skills. This system motivates practitioners and recognizes their progress.

Forms, or hyung, are a key component of Kuk Sool Won. These prearranged sequences of movements teach coordination, balance, and muscle memory. Practitioners perform forms to develop precision and fluidity in their techniques. Each form has a specific pattern and purpose, helping practitioners understand the application of techniques. Forms also connect practitioners to the historical and cultural aspects of Kuk Sool Won.

Self-defense techniques in Kuk Sool Won are practical and effective. Practitioners learn to respond to various threats with strikes, blocks, joint locks, throws, and pressure points. Training includes situational awareness and escape techniques. The emphasis is on using the minimum force necessary to neutralize the threat. Practitioners develop confidence and readiness through regular practice.

Weapons training is another important aspect of Kuk Sool Won. Practitioners learn to handle traditional Korean weapons such as swords, staffs, spears, and knives. Weapons training enhances coordination, precision, and understanding of martial principles. It also connects practitioners to the historical and cultural heritage of Korean martial arts. Proper handling and maintenance of weapons are emphasized.

The healing arts in Kuk Sool Won focus on maintaining and improving health. Practices include acupressure, massage therapy, herbal medicine, breathing exercises, meditation, stretching, diet, hydration, injury prevention, and recovery techniques. These practices ensure that practitioners care for their bodies and minds. The holistic approach to health promotes overall well-being and supports martial arts training.

Modern applications and adaptations of Kuk Sool Won ensure its relevance today. Practitioners learn to handle current threats and incorporate modern training equipment and fitness principles. Technology, such as video analysis, enhances learning. Self-defense seminars, women's self-defense programs, and corporate training workshops address contemporary needs. Online resources and social media connect practitioners globally.

Kuk Sool Won's presence in popular culture has increased its visibility. Films, television shows, documentaries, and video games feature Kuk Sool Won techniques. Books, magazines, and online articles provide valuable information. Public demonstrations, competitions, and celebrity endorsements raise awareness. Social media platforms and community outreach programs engage a broader audience.

The benefits of practicing Kuk Sool Won extend beyond physical skills. Training improves mental attributes such as focus, discipline, and resilience. The philosophical principles foster personal growth and a positive attitude. The sense of community among practitioners provides support and motivation. Kuk Sool Won promotes a balanced and harmonious way of living.

Instructors play a crucial role in Kuk Sool Won training. They provide guidance, feedback, and support to students. Instructors emphasize proper technique, discipline, and respect. Their knowledge and experience are essential for the progress and success of practitioners. The relationship between instructors and students is built on mutual respect and trust.

Kuk Sool Won is suitable for people of all ages and abilities. Children, adults, and seniors can benefit from its practice. Each age group has different needs and goals, and training can be adapted accordingly. Children develop focus, discipline, and self-confidence. Adults improve fitness, stress management, and self-defense skills. Seniors enhance mobility, balance, and mental sharpness.

The holistic approach of Kuk Sool Won encompasses physical, mental, and spiritual development. Practitioners learn to integrate these aspects into their training and daily lives. This balanced approach promotes overall health and well-being. The emphasis on both martial techniques and healing arts ensures comprehensive development.

Regular practice and dedication are essential for success in Kuk Sool Won. Practitioners must commit to consistent training to progress and improve. The journey of learning Kuk Sool Won is ongoing, with continuous opportunities for growth and development. Perseverance and a positive attitude are crucial for achieving goals.

Kuk Sool Won fosters a sense of community and mutual support among practitioners. Training together builds strong bonds and a shared sense of purpose. Community events, seminars, and social activities enhance this sense of belonging. The supportive environment encourages practitioners to achieve their best.

The future of Kuk Sool Won is promising, with ongoing efforts to preserve its traditions while embracing modern adaptations. The martial art continues to evolve, maintaining its relevance in a changing world. The global community of practitioners ensures that Kuk Sool Won will thrive and grow. The commitment to excellence and the holistic approach will sustain its popularity.

In conclusion, Kuk Sool Won is a multifaceted martial art that combines traditional techniques with modern applications. Its emphasis on holistic development, including physical, mental, and spiritual aspects, sets it apart. The structured training, philosophical foundations, and community support foster personal growth and well-being. Understanding and practicing Kuk Sool Won provides a comprehensive and enriching martial arts experience. The continued evolution and adaptation of Kuk Sool Won ensure its enduring appeal and relevance. Practitioners benefit from a balanced and integrated approach to martial arts, making Kuk Sool Won a unique and valuable practice.

Bibliographic Reference

→ Suh, In Hyuk. *Kuk Sool Won: Traditional Korean Martial Arts*. Houston: World Kuk Sool Association, 2003.

→ Yi, Kwang-Su. *The History of Korean Martial Arts*. Seoul: Yonhap Press, 1998.

→ Park, Jae Sang. *Kuk Sool Won: The Path to Mastery*. New York: Martial Arts Media, 2011.

→ Kim, Min Jae. *The Philosophy of Kuk Sool Won*. Busan: Hanul Publishing, 2015.

→ Choi, Yong-Soo. *Comprehensive Guide to Kuk Sool Won Techniques*. Chicago: Dojang Publications, 2007.

→ Lee, Byung Moo. *Kuk Sool Won: Weapons Training and Techniques*. Los Angeles: Martial Arts Press, 2009.

→ Suh, In Joo. *Advanced Kuk Sool Won Forms and Patterns*. Houston: World Kuk Sool Association, 2014.

→ Kim, Hyun Woo. *The Healing Arts of Kuk Sool Won*. Seoul: Budo Press, 2016.

→ Lee, Jin Suk. *Martial Arts and Healing: The Kuk Sool Won Approach*. New York: Health and Martial Arts, 2012.

→ Chung, Tae Sun. *Korean Martial Arts: Tradition and Modernity*. London: Routledge, 2018.

→ Park, Yong Jin. *The Complete Kuk Sool Won*. San Francisco: Martial Arts Publishing, 2010.

→ Jeong, Woo Bin. *Kuk Sool Won in the Modern World*. Boston: Harvard University Press, 2020.

→ Suh, In Hyuk. *The Essence of Kuk Sool Won*. Houston: World Kuk Sool Association, 2005.

→ Kim, Soo Mi. *Women in Kuk Sool Won: Empowerment through Martial Arts*. Seoul: Mirae Media, 2017.

→ Cho, Sang Hyun. *Kuk Sool Won for Kids: A Guide for Young Practitioners*. Chicago: Family Martial Arts Press, 2013.

→ Lee, Kyung Ho. *Mind and Body: The Kuk Sool Won Philosophy*. Los Angeles: Mindful Martial Arts, 2011.

→ Suh, In Hyuk. *Kuk Sool Won: Sparring and Self-Defense Techniques*. Houston: World Kuk Sool Association, 2008.

→ Park, Jung Woo. *Kuk Sool Won Forms and Patterns: A Step-by-Step Guide*. New York: Martial Arts Media, 2014.

→ Shin, Dong Hyun. *The Art and Science of Kuk Sool Won*. London: Martial Arts Studies, 2019.

→ Choi, Mi Sun. *Cultural Heritage of Korean Martial Arts*. Seoul: Korean History Press, 2015.

Author: Whalen Kwon-Ling

The Wise and Witty Master

At 85 years young, Whelan Kwon-Ling is still kicking (literally!). This charming and wise martial arts master has spent his life perfecting his craft and sharing his passion with others. Currently residing in China, the mecca of martial arts, Master Whelan is living his best life, teaching students and writing books that inspire and delight.

A Life of Adventure

Born in Ireland, Master Whelan grew up with a love for storytelling and a penchant for getting into mischief. He discovered his passion for martial arts at a young age and has been hooked ever since. His journey took him to Korea, where he trained in the rigorous art of Korean martial arts, and eventually to China, where he delved into the ancient teachings of Tai Chi, Qigong, and Kung Fu.

Teaching with Heart and Humor

Master Whelan's teaching style is a unique blend of patience, humor, and tough love. He believes in pushing his students to be their best, while also making them laugh and enjoy the journey. His classes are a proof to his energy and enthusiasm, and his students adore him for it.

Author and Storyteller

Master Whelan's writings are a reflection of his warm and engaging personality. His books are filled with stories, anecdotes, and wisdom gained from a lifetime of experience. He writes with a twinkle in his eye and a heart full of love for the martial arts.

Legacy and Impact

Master Whelan's impact on the martial arts community is immeasurable. His teachings have inspired countless students, and his books have become a staple in martial arts literature. He's a true master of his craft, and his legacy will live on through the countless lives he's touched.

Come Learn from the Master

If you're looking for a martial arts journey that's equal parts fun, challenging, and inspiring, come learn from Whelan Kwon-Ling. His writings and teachings will guide you on a path of self-discovery, empowerment, and mastery — with a healthy dose of humor and humility thrown in for good measure!

www.ingramcontent.com/pod-product-compliance
Lightning Source LLC
Chambersburg PA
CBHW071038120226
39585CB00008B/201